How Plants Live and Grow

Henry Abbott

ROSEN
COMMON CORE
READERS

Rosen Classroom™

New York

Published in 2013 by The Rosen Publishing Group, Inc.
29 East 21st Street, New York, NY 10010

Book Design: Michael Harmon

Photo Credits: Cover Elenamiv/Shutterstock.com; p. 4 © iStockphoto.com/hartcreations; pp. 5, 14 Sofiaworld/Shutterstock.com; pp. 6, 16 szefei/Shutterstock.com; p. 7 Reinhold Leitner/Shutterstock.com; p. 8 TITIPONG JUNKAWEEKOOL/Shutterstock.com; pp. 9, 11 DUSAN ZIDAR/Shutterstock.com; p. 10 Dreamframer/Shutterstock.com; p. 12 © iStockphoto.com/redmal; p. 13 (roots) Alena Brozova/Shutterstock.com; p. 13 (carrots) David P. Smith/Shutterstock.com; p. 15 DenisNata/Shutterstock.com; p. 17 ANP/Shutterstock.com; p. 18 Andrew L./Shutterstock.com; p. 19 Comstock/Comstock Images/Getty Images; p. 20 mycola/Shutterstock.com; p. 21 Dmitriy Shironosov/Shutterstock.com.

ISBN: 978-1-4488-8770-5
6-pack ISBN: 978-1-4488-8771-2

Manufactured in the United States of America

CPSIA Compliance Information: Batch #WS12RC: For further information contact Rosen Publishing, New York, New York at 1-800-237-9932.

Word Count: 188

Contents

What kinds of things do you see outside?
You might see plants.

Plants are living things
that grow in the ground.

Plants can't move or talk, but they're alive.

Some plants are very big.
Others are very small.

Most plants start out as a seed. Seeds don't look like plants at all!

You can put the seed in a pot or in the ground.

We cover the seed with dirt
to keep it safe.

The seed needs water and sun.
This helps it grow.

First, the seed grows roots.
Roots take in water.

Some plants have many small roots.
Other plants have one long root.

Seeds grow into baby plants.
These are called sprouts.

The stem grows first.
Stems make plants tall.

Next, plants grow leaves.
Some leaves are big.
Some leaves are small.

All leaves love the sun!

Leaves use the sun to make food.

Sometimes, plants grow flowers.
Flowers smell really good!

You can eat some kinds of plants.
They are called fruits and vegetables.

I like looking at plants.
They make our world pretty.

Do you like plants?
What plants do you have at home?

How a Plant Grows

A seed goes into the ground.

The seed grows roots.

The seed turns into a sprout.

The stem grows above the ground.

Leaves grow from the stem.

The plant grows a flower.

Words to Know

flower

fruit

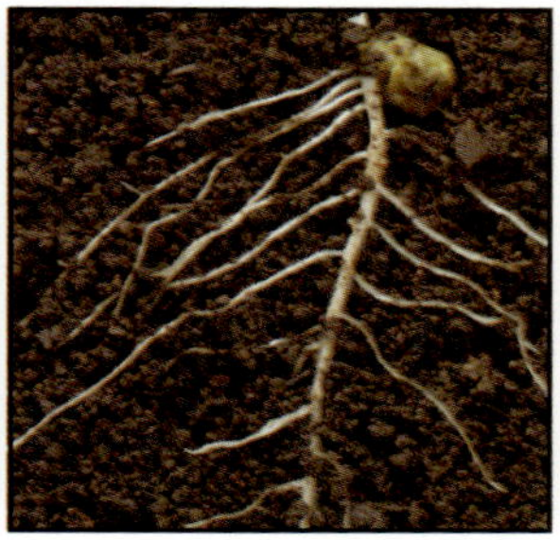

roots

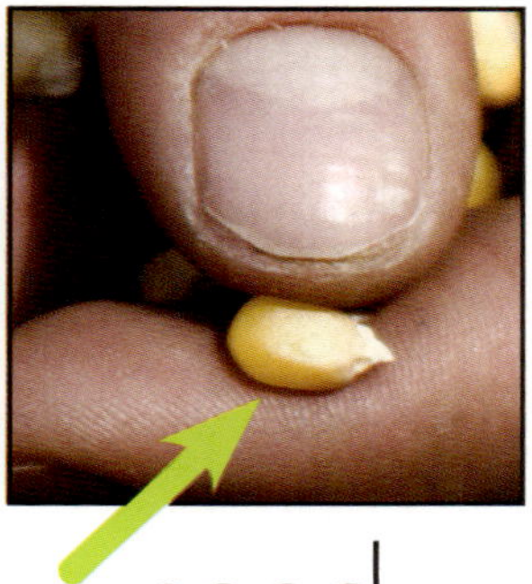

seed

sprout

stem

vegetable

Index